BIGGER BETTER

BIGGER BUSINESS WITH BETTER RESULTS

BY:
JON ROBERT QUINN

Introduction

Welcome! My name is Jon Robert Quinn. I am a business owner, investor, and musician, and I am thrilled to share with you the strategies and insights that have significantly enhanced my Wealth, Health, and Life. This book is not a guide to getting rich quick. Instead, it's a detailed account of the practical methods I have used to transition from a stagnant, go-nowhere job to establishing successful businesses and paving a robust path to financial prosperity.

Throughout this journey, I've learned that building wealth is about more than just accumulating money. It's about creating a solid financial foundation, adopting a strategic mindset, and leveraging the right opportunities. This book is designed to help you understand how to take control of your finances, explore various investment vehicles, and, most importantly, craft a life that aligns with your aspirations.

My Journey

Like many of you, I once found myself trapped in a monotonous job that offered little satisfaction or future prospects. The decision to break free from this cycle was not easy, but it was the most crucial step I took towards financial independence. Through trial and error, persistence, and a lot of learning, I discovered effective methods to start and grow businesses that not only generated income but also provided a sense of fulfillment and purpose.

Building Wealth

In the pages that follow, I will share with you the steps I took to get my finances in order. From budgeting and saving to investing wisely, every chapter is packed with actionable advice and real-life examples. You will learn about different investment vehicles, such as stocks, real estate, and other assets, and how to choose the ones that best suit your financial goals.

Enhancing Health

Wealth without health is meaningless. I will also delve into the practices I've adopted to maintain and improve my health. These are not just physical health tips but also strategies for mental well-being. After all, a healthy mind and body are fundamental to achieving and enjoying long-term success.

Living a Fulfilling Life

Lastly, this book will explore ways to enrich your life beyond financial gains. True wealth includes happiness, personal growth, and the ability to give back to others. I will discuss how to balance work and personal life, the importance of continuous learning, and the joy of contributing to your community.

Your Journey Begins Here

As you read through this book, I encourage you to reflect on the lessons and think about how you can apply them to your own life. The strategies outlined here are not one-size-fits-all; they are meant to inspire and guide you to find your unique path to wealth and fulfillment.

Remember, only YOU have the power to decide your future. Take these lessons to heart, adapt them to your circumstances, and start building the life you desire. Your journey to wealth, health, and a fulfilling life begins now.

So, sit back, relax, and let's embark on this transformative journey together.

Transforming Your Career

Most people hate their job. A lot of people love their job. The difference lies in those who have done their homework and found something that works for them. If you're ready to get rid of your job and start a business, whether it's working from home or opening a restaurant, then listen up.

You get up every morning and think, "Why do I go to work?" Well, it's simple! You must eat. You must feed your family. You must live somewhere, and you want nice things. So, you put up with it. Every single day. But what if it could be different? You're probably thinking to yourself, "I don't have time." Whether you're young or old, have a family or not, there is time to start a business or do something that YOU want to do.

You need to start with you. It's called organization. You need to organize your life to increase your productivity, finance, and health. I will talk about organization throughout this book.

My Personal Journey

I remember when I was working at Office Max for minimum wage. I was working eight hours a day on my feet, taking home something like $1,200 per month. It was crazy. I remember my boss telling me that she had never used a resume to get a job. Maybe that's why she was in her mid-forties and working in customer service. I knew this wasn't what I wanted to do. I wanted to play music. I wanted to tour. I wanted to write records and become somebody.

One day, I came into work, and one of my co-workers said, "Hey, I saw you were showcased on Bearshare. I heard your music. Not bad." That was a huge accomplishment for me. This was an international website that showcased musicians from around the world. I knew about being showcased on the site but never thought in a million years that a co-worker of mine at Office Max would see me online, listen to my music, and acknowledge me as a musician. I knew at that point what I needed to be doing.

Making the Leap

Immediately, I started booking shows at every venue I could. It didn't matter if it was local or out of town, for pay or for free. I knew I needed to be playing, producing, and performing my music. I remember filling out so many time-off requests that the little box on my boss' office door was overflowing with days I couldn't work because I was playing shows somewhere. She came up to me one day and said, "You're going to have to decide whether you're going to work here or play music. You can't do both." I chose music and never looked back.

This is a prime example of figuring out what you want to do and doing it. We all have something special inside of us. What are you passionate about?

Finding Your Passion

Discovering what you are passionate about is the first step toward leaving a job you hate and creating a life you love. It's not about quitting your job on a whim but about finding something that excites you and pursuing it with dedication and strategy. Here are some steps to help you transition from a job you dislike to a fulfilling career or business:

1. **Self-Assessment**: Take time to evaluate your interests, skills, and values. What activities make you lose track of time? What are you naturally good at?

2. **Research**: Look into various career paths or business opportunities that align with your passions. Talk to people already in those fields, read books, and join online forums.

3. **Plan**: Create a detailed plan outlining the steps you need to take to transition from your current job to your desired career or business. This might include further education, networking, or saving money to fund your new venture.

4. **Start Small**: Begin working on your passion project part-time while still employed. This will allow you to test the waters without the financial pressure of immediately replacing your income.

5. **Stay Organized**: As mentioned earlier, organization is key. Keep track of your progress, set milestones, and regularly review your plan to ensure you are on track.

6. **Persevere**: The journey to a fulfilling career or successful business is not always smooth. Be prepared for setbacks and stay committed to your goals.

Conclusion

Your job does not have to define you. With organization, planning, and dedication, you can transition to a career or business that brings you joy and fulfillment. Remember, it starts with you and your willingness to take control of your future. What are you passionate about? Start there and let that passion guide you to a life where work is not a burden but a source of satisfaction and pride.

The Power of Organization

Organization is nothing more than putting something in its place. It's about creating a system that allows you to find what you need when you need it, and to utilize your resources—time, energy, money—efficiently. Let's start with something we all have: a closet. Begin by putting your pants on one side and your shirts on the other side. Place your socks in one drawer and your underwear in another drawer. That's it! That's all it takes to start organizing.

Organizing Your Time

When I talk about getting out of your dead-end job, the first step is organizing your time. It's your time, and you need some of it for yourself! Many people make excuses like, "I don't have time for this or that," but you need to prioritize what YOU need to be happy.

Consider your daily routine: you get up in the morning, get the kids ready, go to work, come home, feed the kids, bathe them, get them in bed, and then you're tired. You follow this routine for years and never leave that dead-end job. Try this instead: when you get home and the TV is on, get a piece of paper and make a list of things you would love to do for a living. Be realistic; an astronaut, while possible, requires decades of training.

Creating Your List

After you have created your list, check off the items that don't really interest you. This is where you decide what it is you want to do. Do you want to work in the medical field? Or law enforcement? What about clothing and fashion?

Maybe photography? Or do you really love purses or fixing things? Every day, start putting a little time, maybe just a half hour, into that goal. As you become more involved, dedicate more time to it. Get the kids involved—if they enjoy it, you'll increase your productivity and spend more quality time with your family.

Taking Steps Toward Your Goal

Let's say you chose the medical field. There are plenty of online classes that work around your schedule, and in a couple of years, you could have a degree that will help you get a job you'd like. If you wanted to start a business, maybe you've always wanted to design clothing. First, find out exactly what aspect of clothing design interests you. Then you need to take action.

Start by making just a few pieces at a time. The kids might help you, and when the clothes are done, they might want to wear them to school. Their friends will see the new clothes and might want some too. As popularity builds, start attending local trade shows and festivals. These events are usually on weekends, so you don't have to take much time off work. All it takes is organization.

The Power of Organization

Organization allows you to systematically approach your goals. Whether it's sorting your closet or restructuring your life, the principles are the same. Here are some key steps to get started:

1. **Prioritize Your Tasks**: Make a list of what needs to be done and rank them in order of importance.
2. **Create a Schedule**: Allocate specific times for each task. Stick to this schedule as closely as possible.

3. **Set Realistic Goals**: Break your ultimate goal into smaller, manageable tasks. This makes the process less overwhelming and allows you to see progress.
4. **Eliminate Distractions**: Identify what diverts your attention and find ways to minimize these distractions.
5. **Utilize Tools**: Use planners, apps, or other tools to help you stay on track.

Conclusion

By organizing your life, you can free up time and energy to pursue your passions and transform your career. Start small, stay consistent, and gradually increase your efforts. Organization is not a one-time event but a continuous process that adapts as your needs and goals evolve. With a structured approach, you can break free from a job you dislike and move toward a fulfilling and prosperous future.

Launch Your First Business

Starting a business is easy. And depending on what it is you want to start, it's fairly inexpensive. Small business loans are available if you want to open a small restaurant, and investors love to get involved in new projects when presented to them. That's what they do, invest.

Now, I'm not saying anybody can start a business, because they cannot. It takes passion, determination, a lot of patience, and a lot of hard work. Even though it's hard work, it doesn't seem like it if you're enjoying what you do. So, how do you start your first business?

The Pursue of Purses

Let's say you love purses. You walk into a store, see a cute purse, and go "OOOH, I want that." And usually, you end up buying it. There are two ways to look at this: you work for somebody else, hate your job, but you're shopping for purses. Let's use that time and turn play into business.

Companies all over the world sell purses, from designer brands to no-name brands. Find a distributor that sells purses. You can do this by looking up Purse Distributors in a search engine. Call them up and ask for a dealer application. Most likely, you will need a business license and seller's permit before creating an account as a dealer with that distributor. Go to your local City Hall for the business license. It shouldn't cost you any more than sixty dollars. The seller permit you can get from your Board of Equalization office. They usually don't cost anything. Once you get your permits, fill out the dealer application, send it to the distributor, and voila. You're now a dealer. Now it's time to sell. Start small. Buy two or three to make sure the quality is there first. You don't want to sell junk to your customers. You'll make a couple of bucks, but they won't come back to buy anything else. When the product arrives, if you're happy with the quality, show it to your friends. You may sell a few or even more to your friends and family. When you have decided that you're 1) having fun and 2) making money, it's time to make a larger purchase.

Organization Is Key

Before you go any further, make sure you're organized. You need a place to work. Do you have a place you can work and keep track of receipts, invoices, and expenses? You need a small desk in the corner of your home where you can work and actually get things done.

You need to separate expenses from sales invoices and so on. Pick up a small business software package from your local office supply store or you can do what I did and build your own.

Taking the Plunge

If you put an hour a day into the business, after a couple of months, you'll see a steady increase in sales if you build a solid foundation. I will talk to you about that shortly.

So, you just got home from work and there is a big box on your porch that contains twenty-four purses. You can't wait to open it. What are you going to do with all those purses? That's easy! Sell them. Flea Markets, online classified ads, and many other avenues are ways YOU can sell that product. Remember, the faster you sell them, the more money that goes into your pocket and quicker you can order more purses. You now own a business. Congratulations.

My First Retail Venture

I remember sitting at home one night and getting the crazy idea of opening a retail store. I already had dozens of online stores selling motorcycle gear, and my apartment literally had hundreds of items I would be taking to local flea markets and selling on Craigslist. I literally had two to three people per day coming by my home to pick up gear, so a retail store was inevitable.

The Initial Hurdles

The first challenge was getting the capital needed and finding a good storefront. Retail space is very expensive, and the last thing we want to do is go out of business before we are actually in business. I scoured Craigslist looking at retail space, and the cheapest place I could find was about eight hundred square feet for around one thousand two hundred dollars per month.

Building a retail store requires attention to ROI (return on investment). ROI is simple. If you invest one thousand two hundred dollars per month into a space, the space must create a return equal to or greater than your cost of the space. My recommendation is two-to-one. Meaning, if you spend one thousand two hundred dollars per month, the space should create a return of two thousand four hundred dollars per month net or after expenses.

A Strategic Decision

Instead of opening a traditional retail store, I opted to rent some commercial office space for under four hundred dollars per month. The space was much smaller and in a strip mall, which was harder to find and less retail-looking, but my return would cover the expenses of rent, electricity, internet, phone, etc. This turned out to be a smart move and an instant success for my customers. Several other stores would soon follow suit.

Building retail stores was a challenge, but a fun challenge. I want to use the space below to show you how to properly design and build your business structure. It's all about leveraging your money and guaranteeing a return.

Product Strategy

Above, you see a variety of products with our unit cost, retail price, and profit. Now a couple of things I want to point out. Sales will obviously affect your profit margins, as well as theft, and taxes paid to the IRS. You also have to factor in the cost of doing business, i.e., employees, rent, etc., but this is a general idea.

Now obviously, it makes sense to sell the more expensive item because you'll make more money on that item. However, not every customer wants to spend hundreds of dollars during one purchase. So, those clients will want a product of maybe a little lesser quality but something that will fit their budget. Flipping the coin, there are customers who absolutely want the more expensive product and will pay full retail for it.

Understanding Your Customers

There are three types of customers: the Dollar Store Customer, the Wal-Mart Customer, and the Nordstrom Customer. All three customers are shoppers and buyers in your store, however, their wants and needs are different. The Dollar Store customer doesn't make a ton of money and wants whatever will get the job done for as little money as possible. The Wal-Mart Customer wants a good product, not superior, and wants it for a fair price. They won't buy the cheapest product but also aren't interested in the top of the line either. The Nordstrom customer may make the same money as the Wal-Mart shopper but will take their time and buy the best they can get because they feel like they deserve it. Some Nordstrom customers make more money than the Wal-Mart shopper and simply don't care about price.

Catering to All Customers

When pricing your products and building your store, make sure you have products available for each of those customers. You want all of them in your store. However, when that Nordstrom customer is buying your product, this is a fantastic time to upsell them with VALUE, meaning, you can sell them additional products of lesser quality, and they feel like they are getting more for less. This also works with your Wal-Mart customers with small ten-dollar add-ons. By showing the benefits of accessories, both The Wal-

Mart and Nordstrom customer will most likely spend more on additional products. This increases your point of sale transaction amount, increasing the health of your business.

Business Infrastructure

As I mentioned earlier, building a business is simple, but it requires time and effort. To create a thriving business, you must establish a solid foundation, often referred to as a business system. This system is crucial for ensuring that every transaction proceeds smoothly and accurately. Without a well-defined system, your business is destined to fail.

Setting the Stage

The system begins even before your first sale. It starts with how you invoice your customers, how you record sales in your database, and how you organize and file invoices once a sale is completed. Moreover, you must diligently track your expenses. Many people believe it's acceptable to incur losses in the first year of business, but I disagree. If you're already losing money in your first year, then your system is failing you. If you can't turn a profit in your first year, how can you expect to survive five, ten, or fifteen years down the line?

A Practical Example

Let's illustrate this with an example. Suppose you order one dozen pairs of sunglasses at $2 each, intending to sell them for $10 each. At first glance, you might think you'll make a profit of $8 per pair. However, after factoring in shipping costs—let's say $6 for the dozen—your profit per pair reduces to $7.50. But that's not all. You must also consider additional expenses like advertising and rental space if you're selling at a flea market.

Scaling Up

Now, imagine you decide to take twenty dozen sunglasses to the flea market instead of just one. With higher quantities, your costs increase significantly. However, your potential earnings also rise. Let's say you sell all two hundred forty pairs of sunglasses in one day at $5 each. After subtracting expenses, you could walk away with a profit of $568. Not bad for a day's work!

Find Your Niche

Remember, you're not limited to selling sunglasses. This was merely an example. Whatever your passion is, there's a market for it, and you can make money selling the things you love. Personally, I have a passion for music, motorcycles, and cars. Consequently, I've diversified my business to include selling music, motorcycle helmets, accessories, and auto parts. I've sold at flea markets, fairs, festivals, as well as online through numerous websites. By pursuing my interests, I wake up every day excited to work in industries I love.

Establishing a solid foundation for your business is essential for long-term success. By meticulously planning your business structure and diligently managing your finances, you pave the way for sustainable growth and profitability.

Mastering Personal Finance

Before diving into entrepreneurship, it's essential to establish control over your personal finances. Balancing a checkbook might seem rudimentary, but it's the cornerstone of financial management. Like any skill, it takes practice to master. However, once you grasp it, you can leverage it to build personal wealth.

The Road to Financial Mastery

I manage my finances across eleven banks. I didn't start this way; it evolved over time. Each bank account serves a distinct purpose, whether for bill payments, savings goals, or securing my financial future. Money, as they say, is power. Without it, our ability to thrive diminishes. So why live paycheck to paycheck? Having financial reserves provides security against unforeseen emergencies, preventing reliance on credit cards or loans.

Getting Started

Most of us have a bank account, but few diligently track every transaction. Utilizing tools like Microsoft Excel or alternative spreadsheet software, meticulously document every income and expense. Consistency is key; make it a habit to update your records daily. Online banking is helpful, but it's not enough on its own. Combining it with a detailed spreadsheet provides a comprehensive view of your finances, empowering informed decision-making.

Building Wealth

Opening a savings account is paramount. Utilize online banking to automate regular transfers from your checking to savings account. Start small, perhaps with a daily transfer of five dollars. Over time, these incremental amounts accumulate into significant savings. By prioritizing saving, you reinforce the habit of paying yourself first, reducing discretionary spending on non-essentials.

Spendthrifts, Savers, and Investors

In the realm of personal finance, individuals typically fall into three categories: spenders, savers, and investors. Spendthrifts exhaust every cent they receive, perpetuating a cycle of financial instability. Savers prioritize saving but may shy away from investment opportunities. Investors strike a balance, allocating funds towards essential expenses, savings, and investment vehicles like stocks. While some consider stocks risky, so too is frivolous spending without consideration for the future.

By embracing prudent financial habits and adopting an investor mindset, you position yourself for long-term financial success. Building wealth isn't solely about earning more; it's about maximizing the potential of every dollar you earn. Through disciplined spending, strategic saving, and intelligent investing, you pave the way for financial security and prosperity.

The Power of Investing

Investing in stocks offers an exhilarating path to wealth creation, albeit with inherent risks. However, these risks diminish with knowledge and strategic decision-making. Understanding the market's dynamics and a company's fundamentals is paramount to success.

Timing is Everything

To navigate the stock market effectively, one must study trends, scrutinize a company's history, and stay informed about industry developments. Belief in the company's potential is crucial; investing without conviction is akin to navigating blindfolded. Consider the auto industry upheaval in 2009. As companies emerged from bankruptcy, their stock prices plummeted, presenting opportune moments to buy low and sell high.

The Simple Formula: Demand and Price

The principle is straightforward: as demand for a stock increases, so does its price. This principle echoes across various markets, from commodities to consumer goods. When assessing potential investments, prioritize companies with a solid track record. For instance, if a century-old company introduces an innovative product with significant market potential, it's likely to spur demand, thereby increasing stock value.

Leveraging Industry Trends

During the 2009 recession, while many shied away from the auto industry, astute investors capitalized on the sector's resilience. Beyond manufacturers, ancillary businesses like dealership chains and rental companies thrived. Similar opportunities abound in other sectors, such as technology and communications, as the world transitions into the information age.

Utilizing Other People's Money (OPM)

The concept of leveraging OPM is a powerful wealth-building strategy. When funds are limited, one can leverage their value proposition to secure investments. For instance, when founding "The Good Life Show with Jon Robert Quinn," financial constraints led to innovative solutions. By offering businesses affordable advertising spots, the show generated sustainable income without upfront investment. This illustrates the principle of exchanging value for value —a cornerstone of financial success.

Conclusion

Stock market success hinges on informed decision-making, meticulous research, and a willingness to adapt to market dynamics. By understanding industry trends, evaluating company fundamentals, and leveraging OPM, investors can navigate the stock market's complexities with confidence. With strategic planning and prudent risk management, the stock market becomes a vehicle for wealth creation and financial independence.

Entrepreneurial Spirit

Entrepreneurship transcends mere business ownership; it embodies a mindset of seizing opportunities and thriving in dynamic environments. While a business owner may contentedly maintain a single enterprise, an entrepreneur navigates multiple ventures with gusto. They possess a unique ability to extract value from any situation, fuelled by passion, determination, and an unwavering commitment to success.

The Distinction Between Business Owner and Entrepreneur

At its core, entrepreneurship is about taking calculated risks and leveraging them to generate wealth and growth. Unlike the cautious business owner who plays it safe, the entrepreneur dives headfirst into uncharted waters, driven by an insatiable hunger for success. Their portfolio spans diverse industries, reflecting a penchant for innovation and a refusal to be confined by conventional boundaries.

Embracing Creativity and Risk

To embark on the entrepreneurial journey is to embrace creativity, discard limitations, and embrace the unknown. It requires breaking free from the confines of traditional thinking and venturing into unexplored territory. Every challenge becomes an opportunity, every setback a chance to innovate and evolve. This journey demands resilience, adaptability, and an unwavering belief in one's abilities.

Cultivating Personal Wealth and Growth

For the entrepreneur, personal wealth and growth are not just financial metrics but manifestations of their boundless ambition and drive. Their ventures serve as conduits for personal and professional development, propelling them towards new heights of success. While the business owner toils diligently for financial stability, the entrepreneur orchestrates a symphony of ventures, each contributing to their ever-expanding empire.

Embracing the Entrepreneurial Spirit

To embrace entrepreneurship is to embark on a transformative journey—a journey fueled by passion, fueled by determination, and fueled by the relentless pursuit of excellence. It's a journey marked by triumphs and setbacks, victories and defeats, yet through it all, the entrepreneurial spirit perseveres. So, step outside the box, embrace the unknown, and prepare for the exhilarating ride of a lifetime. As an entrepreneur, the world is your canvas, and success your masterpiece.

Leading with Integrity

In the realm of business, leadership is paramount, second only to financial management. As a leader, your ability to inspire respect and loyalty among employees and customers alike is crucial for the success and longevity of your enterprise. However, true leadership transcends mere authority—it embodies integrity, empathy, and a genuine commitment to the well-being of those under your charge.

The Essence of Leadership

Being a leader is not synonymous with exerting control or dominance; rather, it entails fostering a culture of mutual respect, trust, and collaboration. While authority is essential, it should be wielded with humility and empathy.

A leader guides, inspires, and empowers others to reach their full potential, thereby cultivating a dynamic and harmonious work environment.

Nurturing Relationships

Central to effective leadership is the cultivation of meaningful relationships—with employees and customers alike. By demonstrating genuine care and interest in the lives of your team members, you foster a sense of camaraderie and loyalty. Similarly, prioritizing customer satisfaction through personalized gestures fosters brand loyalty and positive word-of-mouth advertising.

Balancing Firmness with Compassion

Leadership necessitates striking a delicate balance between assertiveness and compassion. While it's imperative to uphold standards and policies, it's equally crucial to approach disciplinary matters with empathy and understanding. Constructive feedback, coupled with mentorship and guidance, facilitates employee growth and development while reinforcing organizational values.

Leading by Example

As a leader, your actions speak louder than words. Lead by example, embodying the values and principles you wish to instill in your team. Display integrity, accountability, and professionalism in all your endeavors, serving as a role model for others to emulate. Your commitment to excellence sets the tone for the entire organization, inspiring greatness at every level.

Reflecting on Past Experiences

Reflect on your past experiences as an employee and identify the qualities you admired in your superiors. Use these insights to inform your leadership approach, striving to emulate the positive attributes while addressing any shortcomings. By learning from the past, you can create a supportive and empowering work environment that fosters growth and success.

Cultivating a Culture of Excellence

Ultimately, effective leadership is about fostering a culture of excellence—one characterized by mutual respect, open communication, and unwavering commitment to collective goals. By prioritizing the well-being and development of your team members, you lay the foundation for sustained growth and prosperity. Remember, leadership begins with integrity and flourishes through empathy, compassion, and a steadfast dedication to serving others.

Embrace Originality

For your company to thrive, originality is paramount. Being original means thinking differently, opening your mind to change, and coming up with creative solutions to overcome challenges and build a unique business structure.

The Power of Originality

Originality involves taking your most imaginative and unconventional ideas and finding practical ways to make them work using your skills and resources. Consider how Justin Bieber's unique hairstyle set him apart, or how Baskin Robbins offered an unprecedented thirty-one flavors. Similarly, Dodge distinguished itself with the Hemi engine. The question is: how can you distinguish yourself?

When designing your business model, aim to stand out from the competition.

Step One: Innovate Your Product or Service

Evaluate whether your product or service has been done before. If it has, find ways to improve it. Without differentiation, no matter how much you market it, your offering will always be second best. First, identify a want and need. Without these, there is no market. Once you pinpoint the demand, determine your target market. However, don't limit yourself—experiment in other markets as well. For instance, when Honda released the Element SUV, they targeted young adults, but found that it appealed more to an older demographic.

Step Two: Create a Memorable Name

A creative and memorable name is crucial for success. Brainstorm several business name ideas and gather feedback from friends and family through a poll. While their input is valuable, the final decision should resonate with you. If you don't have an emotional connection to the name, don't use it.

Step Three: Market Innovatively

Originality is vital in marketing your product or service. Consider unique approaches such as creating a catchy jingle, partnering with local charities, celebrities, or restaurants to differentiate yourself from competitors.

Testing Your Ideas

One approach I've found effective is to present my craziest ideas to family or customers. If they respond with a lukewarm, "Hmmm, that might work," it indicates the idea may not be as impactful as it could be. However, if they laugh at how ridiculous the idea seems, I know I'm onto something big. When you have a groundbreaking concept, think even bigger. Work out all the details, numbers, and plans on paper first. If it works there, proceed with confidence.

Conclusion

Originality is the key to setting your business apart. By continually thinking creatively and striving to be different, you can develop a unique brand that stands out in the market. Embrace your most unconventional ideas, refine them, and watch your business flourish.

Create a Seamless Business

As I mentioned before, your business is like a child. Keeping it healthy and thriving relies on the systems you put in place. These systems are the engines that power and maintain every aspect of your business.

The Anatomy of a Business System

A business system comprises numerous moving parts, each working in harmony to ensure the business operates smoothly. Every business should have core systems in place, which must be consistently followed to avoid failure.

A simple example of an effective business system is McDonald's. They offer a straightforward product at a simple price, with unparalleled convenience. However, behind the scenes, McDonald's operates one of the most complex business systems in the world. The key to their success lies in the precise execution of tasks by each employee. If any link in the chain breaks, the system might stall. But with procedures firmly in place, the company continues to run efficiently.

Implementing Systems in Your Business

These principles apply to your business as well. Many small business owners juggle multiple roles—salesperson, landlord, accountant, janitor, warehouse manager, order placer, and shipper—essentially creating a demanding job for themselves rather than a scalable business. For your business to grow, you need to hire people and delegate responsibilities. This means relinquishing control over some, if not many, tasks.

The challenge for small business owners is to avoid becoming enslaved by their creation. This is where building a robust foundation comes into play. This foundation starts with hiring the right people for each task.

Delegating Responsibilities

For your new hires to perform their duties effectively, you must develop a system. As you bring more people on board, the system will naturally become more complex. For your company to run efficiently and profitably, employees' responsibilities must be clearly defined and followed accurately.

In relation to the human body, every organ, muscle, and cell serves a specific purpose to ensure the whole organism functions as it should. None of this would be possible without well-designed systems.

Steps to Build an Effective Business System

1. **Identify Core Processes**: Determine the essential tasks that keep your business running. This includes sales, inventory management, customer service, accounting, and marketing.

2. **Document Procedures**: Clearly document each process. This includes step-by-step instructions, required tools, and expected outcomes. Use checklists and flowcharts to make procedures easy to follow.

3. **Assign Responsibilities**: Clearly define who is responsible for each task. Ensure that every team member understands their role and how it fits into the larger system.

4. **Train Employees**: Provide comprehensive training to ensure that all employees understand the procedures and can execute them competently.

5. **Monitor and Adjust**: Regularly review your systems to identify areas for improvement. Solicit feedback from your team and be prepared to make adjustments as needed.

6. **Implement Technology**: Use software and tools to automate processes where possible. This can increase efficiency and reduce the potential for human error.

Conclusion

Building an effective business system is crucial for long-term success. Just as the human body relies on a complex interplay of systems to function, your business depends on well-designed procedures and competent execution. By establishing clear processes, delegating tasks, and continuously refining your systems, you can create a business that runs efficiently and profitably. This approach not only helps prevent you from becoming overwhelmed but also lays the groundwork for sustainable growth and scalability.

Nurturing Your Business

There's a timeless saying: you must give to receive. You must give respect to get respect. You must give love to get love. And you must invest if you want something in return. The same principles apply to your business. If you don't give your business one hundred percent, it won't give it back. My advice to any business owner is to love your business like a child. It's born, it lives, it thrives, and it even makes you proud. It puts a smile on your face, and sometimes it makes you cry. It's a breathing, living, growing extension of you and someday, like everything in this world, it will die. But, like everything you do, if you love it, cherish it, and raise it to be successful, it will love you back.

The Birth and Growth of Your Business

When your first child was born, what did you expect? You expected good things. You wanted your child to succeed, to fall in love, to eventually have children of their own, to move out, and to care for themselves. A business is no different. If you nurture it properly, it can outlive you, take care of you, and branch out into other ventures, growing into something as strong as its parent company.

Loving Your Business Like a Child

When starting your first business, treat it with the same care and attention you would give a child. This involves:

1. **Dedication and Commitment**: Invest time and energy into your business. Understand its needs and address them diligently.
2. **Continuous Learning**: Just as you would learn about parenting to provide the best for your child, educate yourself continuously about business

management, industry trends, and innovative practices.

3. **Adaptability and Growth**: Foster an environment where your business can adapt and grow. Be prepared to make necessary changes to ensure its success.

4. **Emotional Investment**: Be emotionally invested in your business. Celebrate its successes and learn from its failures.

Expecting Good Things

Just like with a child, expect good things from your business. Set high standards and strive to meet them. Believe in its potential to grow, prosper, and make a positive impact. Your faith in your business will inspire others to believe in it too.

The Lifecycle of a Business

Understand that your business, like any living entity, will have a lifecycle. It will be born, grow, and eventually, it may decline. But if you nurture it properly, its legacy can continue through offshoots, subsidiaries, or new ventures inspired by its success.

Conclusion

By loving and nurturing your business as you would a child, you set the stage for its success. Give it your all, expect the best, and watch it grow into something remarkable. A well-nurtured business not only thrives but also brings fulfillment and joy, much like a beloved child.

Boosting Sales

In today's competitive landscape, many sales organizations make the mistake of constantly pushing for more salespeople instead of improving the skills of their current team. This approach is not only costly but also inefficient. It's akin to discarding an old TV because there's nothing good on, rather than switching to a better cable provider.

The Flawed Approach to Sales Training

A prevalent issue with many sales training programs is their reliance on scripts. While scripts can provide a basic framework, they fail to address the dynamic nature of real-world sales interactions. True salesmanship involves thinking on your feet and being adept at problem-solving.

Training salespeople to memorize scripts does not equip them to handle the diverse challenges they will encounter.

The Real Causes of Poor Sales Performance

Often, poor sales performance stems from a lack of interest or burnout rather than a lack of ability. Most salespeople possess the potential to excel, but the organization's structure and environment can significantly impact their performance. Factors such as inadequate compensation, ineffective marketing, and misaligned organizational focus can create a detrimental atmosphere that hampers sales success.

Sales is inherently a mental game. When salespeople are subjected to fear-driven tactics, their performance suffers. A negative, pressure-filled environment can paralyze their ability to close deals. Unfortunately, many sales organizations prioritize their bottom line over fostering a supportive and positive work culture, leading to high turnover and poor morale.

The Pitfalls of Overworking Salespeople

Another common mistake is overworking salespeople. Expecting them to work ten, twelve, or more hours a day to meet quotas may seem productive, but it often leads to mental fatigue and burnout. This not only diminishes the quality of their work but also fosters resentment towards their jobs. Proper training and encouragement can help sales teams achieve the desired results in fewer hours, allowing them to enjoy a better work-life balance and reducing turnover.

Creating a Supportive Sales Environment

To truly enhance sales performance, organizations need to shift their focus from quantity to quality. Here are some key strategies:

1. **Comprehensive Training**: Move beyond scripts and focus on developing critical thinking and problem-solving skills. Equip salespeople with the tools to handle various scenarios and challenges they may face.

2. **Positive Work Culture**: Cultivate an uplifting and supportive environment. Recognize and reward achievements, provide constructive feedback, and create a sense of camaraderie among the team.

3. **Fair Compensation**: Ensure that compensation packages are competitive and reflect the hard work and dedication of the sales team. Financial security can significantly boost motivation and performance.

4. **Balanced Workload**: Encourage a healthy work-life balance by setting realistic expectations and avoiding excessive workloads. This helps maintain mental clarity and job satisfaction.

5. **Continuous Improvement**: Encourage continuous learning and development. Offer regular training sessions, workshops, and opportunities for professional growth.

Adapting to Change

The solutions to these problems are available, yet many organizations fail to implement them. The sales landscape has evolved, and so must the strategies used to manage and train sales teams. Clinging to outdated methods and mindsets will only hinder progress. By embracing change and focusing on the well-being and development of their salespeople, organizations can achieve sustainable success and build a resilient, high-performing sales force.

In conclusion, improving sales performance starts with properly training and supporting your salespeople. By addressing the root causes of poor performance and creating a positive, nurturing environment, you can empower your team to achieve their full potential and drive your business to new heights.

The Pursuit of Happiness

There's an old saying that money doesn't bring happiness. However, neither does being broke or poor. Understanding the distinction between being broke and being poor is crucial. Poor people often remain in poverty throughout their lives, while broke people might temporarily lack funds due to circumstances but have the potential to recover. Being poor can feel permanent, while being broke is a temporary state.

The Difference Between Broke and Poor

Poor people are often trapped in a cycle of poverty, lacking the resources and opportunities to escape. They are born into poverty and often die in poverty. On the other hand, broke people might have money saved away or face a temporary financial setback. Being broke can be a motivator, fueling the hunger and eagerness to build wealth and achieve financial stability.

Building Your Financial Outlook

Use the tools and strategies outlined in this book to improve your financial situation. It's okay to be broke because it means you're striving for something better. Being broke can push you to work hard and achieve your financial goals. It's important to focus your efforts on building wealth, not on spending money to alleviate temporary sadness or depression.

Redirecting Your Focus

Let's revisit the example of purses. Imagine you hate your job, and your life feels monotonous. Instead of buying a purse to cheer yourself up, consider building a business that can lift you out of that dead-end job. By selling those very same purses to others, you can create a source of income and pave the way to financial independence.

Achieving Happiness Through Purpose

True happiness comes from purpose and fulfillment. When you channel your energy into building something meaningful, like a business, you not only improve your financial situation but also enhance your overall well-being. The satisfaction of achieving your goals and the sense of accomplishment that comes from hard work and determination can bring lasting happiness.

Conclusion

While money alone doesn't guarantee happiness, financial stability can certainly improve your quality of life. By understanding the difference between being broke and being poor, and by using the tools provided in this book, you can work towards a brighter financial future. Instead of spending money to fill a void, invest in building a life that brings you genuine joy and fulfillment.

60-Minute Success

In the following chapters, I want to dig deep into becoming successful in your business or career. The previous chapters helped you understand personal finance and building a business. Now it's time to get stronger and more efficient.

The Power of Focus

Success doesn't necessarily require long hours of hard work every single day. Sometimes, what you need is a short, focused burst of productive activity. Imagine dedicating just 60 minutes a day to intense, purposeful work on your most important tasks. This approach can yield remarkable results when executed consistently.

Setting Clear Goals

Start by setting clear, achievable goals. Define what success looks like for you. Whether it's increasing sales, expanding your customer base, or launching a new product, having a clear goal provides direction and purpose. Break down your larger goals into smaller, manageable tasks that you can tackle within your 60-minute sessions.

Prioritizing Tasks

Not all tasks are created equal. Prioritize tasks that have the highest impact on your business or career. Use the 80/20 rule, which states that 80% of your results come from 20% of your efforts. Focus on the critical 20% during your dedicated hour. This might include tasks like strategizing, planning, networking, or working on a key project.

Eliminating Distractions

To make the most of your 60 minutes, eliminate distractions. Find a quiet place to work, turn off notifications, and let others know you're not to be disturbed during this time. Concentration is key to making the most of your focused work session.

Utilizing Tools and Techniques

There are various tools and techniques that can help you maximize your productivity during your 60-minute sessions. Consider using the Pomodoro Technique, which involves working for 25 minutes and then taking a 5-minute break. Repeat this cycle four times, then take a longer break. This method can help maintain focus and prevent burnout.

Reflecting and Adjusting

At the end of each 60-minute session, take a few minutes to reflect on what you accomplished. Assess what went well and identify areas for improvement. Adjust your approach as needed to enhance efficiency and effectiveness in future sessions.

Consistency is Key

Consistency is crucial for achieving success. Dedicate 60 minutes each day to focused, productive work. Over time, these small increments of dedicated effort will accumulate, leading to significant progress and success in your business or career.

Conclusion

The 60-minute success strategy is about making the most of your time through focused, purposeful activity. By setting clear goals, prioritizing tasks, eliminating distractions, utilizing effective techniques, and maintaining consistency, you can achieve remarkable results. This approach helps you become stronger and more efficient, paving the way for sustained success in your business or career.

Mastering Auto Sales

In this chapter, I want to delve into the world of auto sales, a topic that resonates deeply with many of my readers and listeners in the car business. I extend my gratitude to them and offer some valuable insights to further enhance their skills and strategies.

The Challenges of Auto Sales

The car business is undeniably tough. I've been there, spending countless hours on the showroom floor, often eating dinner at midnight while waiting for customers to finish up in finance. However, the stress and frustration that often accompany auto sales can be mitigated by focusing on customer care and satisfaction.

Building Relationships with Clients

One memorable day, I sold three cars to three different clients, one of whom waited several hours just to work with me. Despite efforts by the sales manager and general manager to assign them to other salespeople, these clients insisted on working with me. The first clients of the day had initially come to see another salesperson but were so turned off by their experience that they were about to leave. I intercepted them as they were getting into their car and turned the situation around.

Turning a Disgruntled Customer into a Loyal Client

Approaching disgruntled customers requires tact and empathy. After assessing the situation, I apologized on behalf of the other salesperson and offered my assistance. They were hesitant at first, but I leveled with them by sharing a similar personal experience. This helped build rapport and trust. I then asked what they were looking for and suggested an option, assuring them they would only work with me.

Not only did I manage to get them back into the showroom, but I also juggled an existing appointment that arrived at the same time. I seated my appointment at a table in front of the newly returned customers and ordered lunch to keep them occupied. This approach not only salvaged the initial sale but also demonstrated my commitment to customer satisfaction.

The Steps of a Successful Sale

Regardless of the product, knowing the steps of a successful sale is crucial:

1. **Greeting**: "Hi, my name is… and you are?"

2. **Walk and Talk**: "How can I help you today? What are you looking for?"

3. **Land**: Guide the client to a product they choose themselves.

4. **Demo**: Highlight features and address their specific needs and wants.

5. **Write Up**: Discuss options, trade-ins, and upsell additional features.

6. **Close**: Ensure the transaction is smooth and the customer leaves happy.

Closing the Deal

In my story, I eventually sold the clients a new truck that exceeded their initial expectations and budget. By emphasizing the benefits and addressing their specific needs, such as power running boards for the wife and a spray-in bed liner for their dirt bikes, I provided value rather than just pushing a sale.

After the first sale, I moved on to my second client, who had enjoyed their complimentary lunch. As I was wrapping up, a previous client returned, insisting on working with me again. This client's loyalty paid off, resulting in another successful sale. My final customer of the day initially came for a grey Chrysler 300 but left with a brown one after some negotiation and demonstrating the value of the vehicle.

The Key to Successful Sales

The key issue many salespeople face is inserting themselves too much into the transaction, forgetting that the focus should be on the customer. Prioritizing the customer's needs and ensuring they have a positive experience will naturally lead to better sales and customer loyalty.

Conclusion

Auto sales don't have to be stressful or resented. By taking care of your clients and focusing on their needs, you can transform your approach and achieve success. Read the next chapter on Sales to gain a deeper understanding of how to improve your sales techniques and build stronger customer relationships.

Mastering the Art of Sales

Sales as a profession isn't easy, but it can be significantly more manageable with a proper understanding of what sales actually entail. By breaking down the core principles of sales and focusing on the essential components, you can enhance your effectiveness and achieve greater success.

The Essence of Sales

My acronym for sales encapsulates the fundamental elements that define a successful sale:

S = Simple

A = And

L = Less

E = Expensive

S = Solutions

A successful sale should be easy for the client, provide cost savings or benefits, and offer a solution to a problem. This approach ensures that the client perceives value and satisfaction in the transaction.

The 3 Ms or 3 Ps of Sales

In addition to the core elements, successful sales also require the presence of two out of three crucial components, often referred to as the 3 Ms or the 3 Ps:

3 Ms:

1. **Man (Person)**
2. **Money (Price)**
3. **Machine (Product)**

3 Ps:

1. Price
2. Person
3. Product

The Dynamics of a Successful Sale

To secure a deal, at least two of these three components must align positively for the client:

1. **Person (Man)**: The client must like and trust you. Building rapport and establishing trust are critical to overcoming objections and closing the sale.

2. **Product (Machine)**: The client must find the product appealing and suitable for their needs. Ensuring that the product meets or exceeds their expectations is essential.

3. **Price (Money)**: The client must perceive the price as fair and reasonable. Offering value for money and demonstrating the benefits justifies the cost.

Applying the 3 Ms/3 Ps

- **If the Client Doesn't Like You (Person)**: Even if the product and price are perfect, a lack of rapport can derail the sale. However, if the product and price are compelling enough, they might overlook their dislike.

- **If the Product Isn't Right (Machine)**: If the client likes you and the price is right, they might still proceed with the purchase, banking on your credibility and the deal's value.

- **If the Price Isn't Right (Money)**: If the client likes you and the product, they might be willing to stretch their budget or explore financing options.

Practical Example

Imagine you're selling a high-end kitchen appliance. Here's how the 3 Ms/3 Ps could play out:

1. **Building Rapport (Person)**: Greet the client warmly and engage in conversation to understand their needs. Your friendly demeanor and expertise make them feel comfortable and valued.

2. **Showcasing the Product (Machine)**: Demonstrate the appliance's features and benefits, highlighting how it solves a specific problem or enhances their

lifestyle. Let them interact with the product to build excitement and confidence.

3. **Justifying the Price (Money)**: Present the price in a way that emphasizes the value and long-term savings. Offer comparisons with competitors to show why your product is the best choice.

If the client is hesitant about the price but loves the product and trusts you, they're more likely to negotiate or seek financing. If they're unsure about the product but like you and find the price reasonable, your credibility can tip the scales in your favor.

Conclusion

Mastering the art of sales involves understanding and implementing these core principles. By ensuring simplicity, providing value, and offering solutions, you can make the sales process easier and more satisfying for your clients.

Remember, the key to closing a deal lies in aligning at least two out of the three critical components—Person, Product, and Price. With this approach, you can build stronger client relationships, increase your closing rate, and achieve lasting success in sales.

The Art of Smile and Dial

Cold calling—those two words can strike fear into the hearts of even the most seasoned sales professionals. However, when executed correctly, cold calls can be the most effective form of marketing, opening doors to countless opportunities. In this chapter, we'll delve into the art of cold calling, providing you with a step-by-step guide to maximize your efficiency and results.

The Power of Smile and Dial

Cold calling is often synonymous with rejection and frustration, but it doesn't have to be. With the right approach and mindset, you can turn cold calls into valuable connections and lucrative deals. I call it Smile and Dial—a methodical process that combines persistence, efficiency, and strategic communication to yield exceptional results.

Organizing Your Cold Call Strategy

Before diving into cold calls, it's crucial to organize your approach. Start by creating an Excel spreadsheet to manage your contacts effectively. Divide the spreadsheet into separate sheets alphabetically, allowing you to categorize contacts based on their names.

- **Column A**: First & Last Name
- **Column B**: Type of Business
- **Column C**: Phone Number
- **Column D**: Email Address
- **Column E**: 1st Contact
- **Column F**: 2nd Contact
- **Column G**: 3rd Contact

Utilize color coordination to track the status of each contact:

- **White**: Open (Untouched)
- **Yellow**: Attempted Contact (no contact)
- **Orange**: Made Contact / Interested
- **Burgundy**: No Contact after 4 attempts / Not Interested
- **Red**: DNC (Do Not Contact)
- **Blue**: Sold (Invoice Sent / Not Paid)
- **Green**: Closed (Paid)

Implementing Efficiency in Cold Calling

Efficiency is key to successful cold calling. Follow these guidelines to optimize your efforts:

- **Keep Calls Short**: Aim for each call to last no longer than 15 seconds.

- **Avoid Voicemail**: Never leave a voicemail; it's a time-consuming endeavor with minimal returns.
- **Limit Hold Time**: If the call goes unanswered, hang up promptly and remove the contact from your list.
- **Focus on Contact**: Strive to make direct contact with the intended recipient.

The 3 Ps of Cold Calling

Remember the 3 Ps: Person, Product, and Price. A successful cold call requires at least two of these components to align positively:

1. **Person (Man)**: Build rapport and establish trust with the contact.
2. **Product (Machine)**: Present a compelling product or solution that addresses their needs.
3. **Price (Money)**: Offer competitive pricing or value propositions.

Navigating Conversations Effectively

When making contact, introduce yourself and inquire about the email you sent. Keep the conversation brief and focused, addressing any interest or concerns promptly. Remember to listen to the story behind their responses, rather than just the words spoken.

Managing Follow-Ups and Closures

Follow up with contacts after initial contact, but limit attempts to three. If no deal materializes, mark them as Not Interested and revisit them at a later date. For interested prospects, initiate the sales process and track progress accordingly.

Finding Leads and Expanding Your Network

Leverage networking opportunities to expand your contact list continually. Engage with peers, exchange business cards, and explore mutually beneficial partnerships. Over time, your network will grow, providing a steady stream of leads and opportunities.

Conclusion

Cold calling doesn't have to be daunting. With a structured approach, effective communication, and persistence, you can transform cold calls into valuable connections and lucrative deals. Implement the Smile and Dial strategy, stay organized, and watch as your sales soar.

Social Media Marketing

In today's digital age, marketing has evolved into a multifaceted landscape, encompassing various channels such as social media, traditional media, and word of mouth. Among these, social media stands out as a powerful tool for businesses to connect with their audience and expand their reach. In this chapter, we'll delve into the world of social media marketing and explore strategies to maximize its potential for your business.

The Power of Social Media

Social media platforms like Facebook and Twitter have revolutionized the way businesses interact with their customers. With millions of users worldwide, these platforms offer unparalleled access to potential customers and provide a platform for businesses to showcase their products and services.

Building Your Social Media Presence

The first step in leveraging social media for marketing is to establish a strong presence on relevant platforms. Start by creating a business page on Facebook and optimizing it with relevant information about your business, including your products, services, and contact details.

Growing Your Following

Growing your social media following is essential for expanding your reach and engaging with potential customers. Utilize a two-pronged approach:

1. **Personal Page Interaction**: Friend request new individuals on your personal Facebook page daily to expand your network.

2. **Business Page Promotion**: Invite existing Facebook friends to like and follow your business page, increasing its visibility among your social circle.

Engaging Content Creation

Content is king in the realm of social media marketing. Create compelling and engaging content that resonates with your audience, including:

- **Videos**: Utilize Facebook Live to share video content showcasing your business, products, or customer testimonials.
- **Images**: Share visually appealing images related to your business, such as product photos or behind-the-scenes shots.
- **Written Content**: Craft engaging captions and posts that provide value to your audience and encourage interaction.

Maximizing Reach and Engagement

To maximize the reach and engagement of your social media content, consider the following strategies:

- **Tagging**: Tag relevant individuals or businesses in your posts to increase visibility and encourage shares.

- **Cross-Promotion**: Share your business page posts on your personal page and encourage friends to like and share them.

- **Call to Action**: Include clear calls to action in your posts, directing followers to visit your website or contact you for more information.

Measuring Success

Track the performance of your social media marketing efforts using built-in analytics tools provided by platforms like Facebook. Monitor key metrics such as reach, engagement, and click-through rates to evaluate the effectiveness of your strategies and make data-driven decisions moving forward.

Conclusion

Social media marketing presents unparalleled opportunities for businesses to connect with their audience, build brand awareness, and drive sales. By leveraging the power of platforms like Facebook and Twitter and implementing effective strategies for content creation and engagement, you can establish a strong online presence and propel your business to new heights of success.

Entrepreneurial Journey

As we reach the conclusion of this book, I want to emphasize the importance of maintaining a mindset of growth and adaptation in your entrepreneurial journey. Let's delve into what it means to stay "Green" and reflect on the lessons learned along the way.

The Significance of Staying Green

To stay "Green" is to remain eager to learn, grow, and evolve in the ever-changing landscape of entrepreneurship. It's about embracing new challenges, seeking out opportunities for innovation, and continuously striving for improvement. In essence, it's the key to staying relevant and competitive in today's dynamic business world.

Embracing Success and Failure

Over the course of my 20-year entrepreneurial journey, I've experienced both success and failure. And I've come to realize that both are invaluable teachers. Success celebrates our victories and reinforces our strategies, while failure offers crucial lessons and insights that propel us forward. Embracing both success and failure allows us to learn, adapt, and ultimately grow stronger as entrepreneurs.

The Cost of Education

In the realm of entrepreneurship, education comes in many forms. Some pursue formal education through college degrees, while others, like myself, embark on a journey of hands-on learning through trial and error. While the path may differ, the lessons learned are equally valuable. Every success and failure, every challenge overcome, contributes to our growth and development as entrepreneurs.

Embracing the Entrepreneurial Spirit

Above all, entrepreneurship is a journey of passion, innovation, and resilience. It's about seizing opportunities, overcoming obstacles, and daring to pursue our dreams. As entrepreneurs, we must embrace the entrepreneurial spirit within us, harnessing our creativity and resourcefulness to navigate the challenges ahead.

Conclusion

In conclusion, I encourage you to embrace the entrepreneurial journey with enthusiasm and determination. Stay "Green" in your pursuit of knowledge and growth, and never shy away from the lessons that success and failure have to offer. Remember to innovate, adapt, and always use your head over your back. With dedication and perseverance, the possibilities are limitless in the world of entrepreneurship. So go forth, embark on your journey, and let your entrepreneurial spirit soar.

www.ingramcontent.com/pod-product-compliance
Lightning Source LLC
Chambersburg PA
CBHW052331220526
45472CB00001B/369